Java Parsing
Collection XML JSON

YANG HU

Simple is the beginning of wisdom. From the essence of practice, this book to briefly explain the concept and vividly cultivate programming interest.

http://en.verejava.com

ISBN: 9781095373378

CONTENTS

Parsing XML Attributes CRUD

If you need to learn Java basics, please read book <<Easy Learning Java>>

https://www.amazon.com/dp/B07Q7MX7Z8

1. Download the jar package for parsing XML

dom4j-1.6.1.jar

jaxen-1.1-beta-6.jar

http://en.verejava.com/download.jsp?id=1

2. Create a student.xml file

```xml
<?xml version="1.0" encoding="UTF-8"?>
<data>
  <student id="1" name="David" age="20">Opportunity Every Day</student>
  <student id="2" name="James" age="21">Life Is Perfect</student>
</data>
```

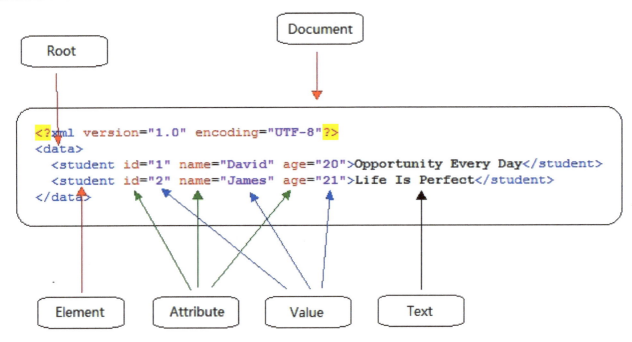

3. Create a new test Java Project in Eclipse, and then add jar to Java Project
dom4j-1.6.1.jar
jaxen-1.1-beta-6.jar

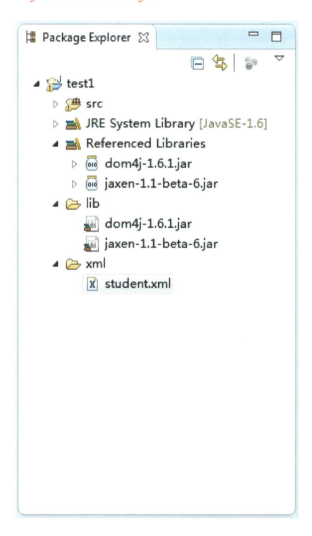

4. Create a TestAdd.java in the project for adding an element to student.xml

```java
import java.io.*;
import java.util.*;
import org.dom4j.*;
public class TestAdd {
    public static void main(String[] args) {
        XMLWriter writer = null;
        try {
            SAXReader reader = new SAXReader();

            //Load student.xml to a Document object
            Document doc = reader.read(new File("xml/student.xml"));

            //Get root element
            Element root = doc.getRootElement();

            //Add a child element of student under the root
            Element studentElement = root.addElement("student");

            //Add attribute
            studentElement.addAttribute("id", "3");
            studentElement.addAttribute("name", "Isacc");
            studentElement.addAttribute("age", "19");

            //Add text
            studentElement.addText("Dream A New Dream");

            writer = new XMLWriter(new FileWriter("xml/student.xml"),
OutputFormat.createPrettyPrint());
            writer.write(doc); //write document to student.xml
            writer.flush();
        } catch (Exception e) {
            e.printStackTrace();
        } finally {
            try {
                writer.close();
            } catch (IOException e) {
                e.printStackTrace();
            }
        }
    }
}
```

Result:

```xml
<?xml version="1.0" encoding="UTF-8"?>

<data>
 <student id="1" name="David" age="20">Opportunity Every Day</student>
 <student id="2" name="James" age="21">Life Is Perfect</student>
 <student id="3" name="Isacc" age="19">Dream A New Dream</student>
</data>
```

5. Create a TestDelete.java for delete element with id=3 from student.xml

```java
import java.io.*;
import java.util.List;
import org.dom4j.*;
public class TestDelete {
  public static void main(String[] args) {
    XMLWriter writer = null;
    try {
      SAXReader reader = new SAXReader();
      Document doc = reader.read(new File("xml/student.xml"));

      //Get all the student elements
      List<Element> elementList = doc. selectNodes("/data/student");
      for (int i = 0; i < elementList.size(); i++) {
        Element element = elementList.get(i);
        if ("3".equals(element.attributeValue("id"))) {
          element.getParent().remove(element);
        }
      }

      writer = new XMLWriter(new FileWriter("xml/student.xml"),
OutputFormat.createPrettyPrint());
      writer.write(doc); //write document to student.xml
      writer.flush();
    } catch (Exception e) {
      e.printStackTrace();
    } finally {
      try {
        writer.close();
      } catch (IOException e) {
        e.printStackTrace();
      }
    }
  }
}
```

Result:

```xml
<?xml version="1.0" encoding="UTF-8"?>
<data>
 <student id="1" name="David" age="20">Opportunity Every Day</student>
 <student id="2" name="James" age="21">Life Is Perfect</student>
</data>
```

6. Create a TestReader.java for read all student element from student.xml

```java
import java.io.File;
import java.util.List;
import org.dom4j.*;

public class TestReader {
    public static void main(String[] args) {
        try {
            SAXReader reader = new SAXReader();
            Document doc = reader.read(new File("xml/student.xml"));

            //Get the student Nodes
            List<Node> nodeList = doc.selectNodes("/data/student");

            for (Node node : nodeList) {
                //Get the value by the attribute
                int id = Integer.parseInt(node.valueOf("@id"));
                String name = node.valueOf("@name");
                int age = Integer.parseInt(node.valueOf("@age"));
                String text = node.getText();

                System.out.println(id + "," + name + "," + age + "," + text);
            }
        } catch (Exception e) {
            e.printStackTrace();
        }
    }
}
```

Result:

Problems @ Javadoc Declaration **Console** ✕

`<terminated>` TestReader [Java Application] C:\Program Files (x86)\Java\jre6\

```
1,David,20,Opportunity Every Day
2,James,21,Life Is Perfect
```

7. Create a TestUpdate.java for update element with id=2 from student.xml

```java
import java.io.*;
import java.util.List;
import org.dom4j.*;
public class TestUpdate {
    public static void main(String[] args) {
        XMLWriter writer = null;
        try {
            SAXReader reader = new SAXReader();
            Document doc = reader.read(new File("xml/student.xml"));

            List<Element> elementList = doc.selectNodes("/data/student");
            for (int i = 0; i < elementList.size(); i++) {
                Element element = elementList.get(i);
                if ("2".equals(element.attributeValue("id"))) {
                    element.setAttributeValue("name", "Make");
                    element.setAttributeValue("age", "25");
                    element.setText("Get Better, Be The Best!");
                }
            }

            writer = new XMLWriter(new FileWriter("xml/student.xml"),
OutputFormat.createPrettyPrint());
            writer.write(doc);
            writer.flush();
        } catch (Exception e) {
            e.printStackTrace();
        } finally {
            try {
                writer.close();
            } catch (IOException e) {
                e.printStackTrace();
            }
        }
    }
}
```

Result:

```xml
<?xml version="1.0" encoding="UTF-8"?>
<data>
 <student id="1" name="David" age="20">Opportunity Every Day</student>
 <student id="2" name="Make" age="25">Get Better, Be The Best!</student>
</data>
```

Parsing XML No Attributes CRUD

1. Create a student2.xml file

```xml
<?xml version="1.0" encoding="UTF-8"?>
<data>
  <student>
    <id>1</id>
    <name>David</name>
    <age>20</age>
  </student>
  <student>
    <id>2</id>
    <name>Grace</name>
    <age>21</age>
  </student>
</data>
```

2. Create a TestAdd.java in the project for adding an element to student2.xml

```java
import java.io.*;
import org.dom4j.*;

public class TestAdd {
    public static void main(String[] args) {
        XMLWriter writer = null;
        try {
            SAXReader reader = new SAXReader();
            Document doc = reader.read(new File("xml/student2.xml"));

            Element root = doc.getRootElement();
            Element studentElement = root.addElement("student");

            //Add a child elements
            Element idElement = studentElement.addElement("id");
            idElement.setText("3");

            Element nameElement = studentElement.addElement("name");
            nameElement.setText("Mathew");

            Element ageElement = studentElement.addElement("age");
            ageElement.setText("30");

            writer = new XMLWriter(new FileWriter("xml/student2.xml"),
OutputFormat.createPrettyPrint());
            writer.write(doc);
            writer.flush();

        } catch (Exception e) {
            e.printStackTrace();
        } finally {
            try {
                writer.close();
            } catch (IOException e) {
                e.printStackTrace();
            }
        }
    }
}
```

Result:

```xml
<?xml version="1.0" encoding="UTF-8"?>
<data>
  <student>
    <id>1</id>
    <name>David</name>
    <age>20</age>
  </student>
  <student>
    <id>2</id>
    <name>Grace</name>
    <age>21</age>
  </student>
  <student>
    <id>3</id>
    <name>Mathew</name>
    <age>30</age>
  </student>
</data>
```

3. Create a TestDelete.java for deleting an element with id=3 from student2.xml

```java
import java.io.*;
import java.util.*;
import org.dom4j.*;

public class TestDelete {
   public static void main(String[] args) {
     XMLWriter writer = null;
     try {
        SAXReader reader = new SAXReader();
        Document doc = reader.read(new File("xml/student2.xml"));
        List<Element> elementList = doc.selectNodes("/data/student");
        for (int i = 0; i < elementList.size(); i++) {
           Element element = elementList.get(i);

           //Get the child element of the student Element
           Iterator<Element> elementIter = element.elementIterator();

           while (elementIter.hasNext()) {
              Element childElement = elementIter.next();
              if ("3".equals(childElement.getText())&&"id".equals(childElement.getName())){
                 element.getParent().remove(element);
                 break;
              }
           }
        }

        writer = new XMLWriter(new FileWriter("xml/student2.xml"),
OutputFormat.createPrettyPrint());
        writer.write(doc);
        writer.flush();
     } catch (Exception e) {
        e.printStackTrace();
     } finally {
        try {
           writer.close();
        } catch (IOException e) {
           e.printStackTrace();
        }
     }
   }
}
```

Result:

```xml
<?xml version="1.0" encoding="UTF-8"?>
<data>
  <student>
    <id>1</id>
    <name>David</name>
    <age>20</age>
  </student>
  <student>
    <id>2</id>
    <name>Grace</name>
    <age>21</age>
  </student>
</data>
```

4. Create a TestUpdate.java for update an element by id=2 in student2.xml

```java
import java.io.*;
import java.util.*;
import org.dom4j.*;
public class TestUpdate {
   public static void main(String[] args) {
      XMLWriter writer = null;
      try {
         SAXReader reader = new SAXReader();
         Document doc = reader.read(new File("xml/student2.xml"));

         List<Element> elementList = doc.selectNodes("/data/student");
         for (int i = 0; i < elementList.size(); i++) {
            Element element = elementList.get(i);
            Iterator<Element> elementIter = element.elementIterator();
            boolean isUpdate = false;
            while (elementIter.hasNext()) {
               Element childElement = elementIter.next();
               if ("2".equals(childElement.getText())&&"id".equals(childElement.getName())){
                  isUpdate = true;
               }

               if (isUpdate) {
                  if ("name".equals(childElement.getName())) {
                     childElement.setText("John");
                  } else if ("age".equals(childElement.getName())) {
                     childElement.setText("50");
                  }
               }
            }
         }
         writer = new XMLWriter(new FileWriter("xml/student2.xml"),
OutputFormat.createPrettyPrint());
         writer.write(doc);
         writer.flush();
      } catch (Exception e) {
         e.printStackTrace();
      } finally {
         try {
            writer.close();
         } catch (IOException e) {
            e.printStackTrace();
         }
```

```
      }
    }
}
```

Result:

```xml
<?xml version="1.0" encoding="UTF-8"?>

<data>
  <student>
    <id>1</id>
    <name>David</name>
    <age>20</age>
  </student>
  <student>
    <id>2</id>
    <name>John</name>
    <age>50</age>
  </student>
</data>
```

5. Create a TestReader.java for read data from student2.xml

```java
import java.io.File;
import java.util.*;
import org.dom4j.*;
public class TestReader {

    public static void main(String[] args) {
        try {
            SAXReader reader = new SAXReader();
            Document doc = reader.read(new File("xml/student2.xml"));

            List<Element> elementList = doc.selectNodes("/data/student");
            for (int i = 0; i < elementList.size(); i++) {
                Element element = elementList.get(i);

                Iterator<Element> elementIter = element.elementIterator();
                while (elementIter.hasNext()) {
                    Element childElement = elementIter.next();
                    System.out.println(childElement.getText());
                }
            }
        } catch (Exception e) {
            e.printStackTrace();
        }
    }
}
```

Result:

```
Problems  @ Javadoc  Declaration  Console ☒

<terminated> TestReader (1) [Java Application] C:\Program Files (x86)\Java\jr
1
David
20
2
John
50
```

16

Convert List to XML File

convert to

```
List
```

```
Department
id : int
name : String
```

```xml
<?xml version="1.0" encoding="UTF-8"?>

<data>
    <department>
        <id>1</id>
        <name>Finance</name>
    </department>
    <department>
        <id>2</id>
        <name>Administration</name>
    </department>
    <department>
        <id>3</id>
        <name>IT</name>
    </department>
</data>
```

1. Create a model class : Department.java

```java
public class Department {
    private int id;
    private String name;

    public Department() {

    }

    public Department(String name) {

        this.name = name;
    }

    public Department(int id, String name) {
        this.id = id;
        this.name = name;
    }

    public int getId() {
        return id;
    }

    public void setId(int id) {
        this.id = id;
    }

    public String getName() {
        return name;
    }

    public void setName(String name) {
        this.name = name;
    }
}
```

2. Create class: TestDeptToXml Convert List to XML

```java
import java.io.*;
import java.util.*;
import org.dom4j.*;
public class TestDeptToXml {
    public static void main(String[] args) {
        List<Department> deptList = new ArrayList<Department> ();
        deptList.add(new Department(1, "Finance"));
        deptList.add(new Department(2, "Administration"));
        deptList.add(new Department(3, "IT"));

        StringBuilder sb = new StringBuilder();
        sb.append("<?xml version=\"1.0\" encoding=\"UTF-8\"?>\n");
        sb.append("<data>\n");
        for (int i = 0; i < deptList.size(); i++) {
            Department dept = deptList.get(i);
            sb.append("   <department>\n");
            sb.append("      <id>" + dept.getId() + "</id>\n");
            sb.append("      <name>" + dept.getName() + "</name>\n");
            sb.append("   </department>\n");
        }
        sb.append("</data>");
        parseXml(sb.toString());
    }

    public static void parseXml(String xml) {
        XMLWriter writer = null;
        try {
            Document doc = DocumentHelper.parseText(xml);
            writer = new XMLWriter(new FileWriter("xml/department.xml"),
OutputFormat.createPrettyPrint());
            writer.write(doc);
            writer.flush();
        } catch (Exception e) {
            e.printStackTrace();
        } finally {
            try {
                writer.close();
            } catch (IOException e) {
                e.printStackTrace();
            }
        }
    }
}
```

Result:

```xml
<?xml version="1.0" encoding="UTF-8"?>

<data>
   <department>
      <id>1</id>
      <name>Finance</name>
   </department>
   <department>
      <id>2</id>
      <name>Administration</name>
   </department>
   <department>
      <id>3</id>
      <name>IT</name>
   </department>
</data>
```

Convert XML to List

```xml
<?xml version="1.0" encoding="UTF-8"?>

<data>
    <department>
        <id>1</id>
        <name>Finance</name>
    </department>
    <department>
        <id>2</id>
        <name>Administration</name>
    </department>
    <department>
        <id>3</id>
        <name>IT</name>
    </department>
</data>
```

convert to

List

Department
id : int
name : String

1. Create class: TestXmlToList Convert XML to List

```java
import java.io.*;
import java.util.*;
import org.dom4j.*;

public class TestXmlToList {
   public static void main(String[] args) {
      List<Department> deptList = xmlToList("xml/department.xml");
      for (int i = 0; i < deptList.size(); i++) {
         Department dept = deptList.get(i);
         System.out.println(dept.getId() + " , " + dept.getName());
      }
   }

   public static List<Department> xmlToList(String fileName) {
      List<Department> deptList = new ArrayList<Department>();
      try {
         SAXReader reader = new SAXReader();
         Document doc = reader.read(new File(fileName));
         List<Element> elementList = doc.selectNodes("/data/department");
         for (int i = 0; i < elementList.size(); i++) {

            Element element = elementList.get(i);
            Department dept = new Department();
            Iterator<Element> elementIter = element.elementIterator();
            while (elementIter.hasNext()) {
               Element childElement = elementIter.next();
               if ("id".equals(childElement.getName())) {
                  dept.setId(Integer.parseInt(childElement.getText()));
               } else if ("name".equals(childElement.getName())) {
                  dept.setName(childElement.getText());
               }
            }
            deptList.add(dept); //Department add to deptList
         }
      } catch (DocumentException e) {
         e.printStackTrace();
      }
      return deptList;
   }
}
```

22

Result:

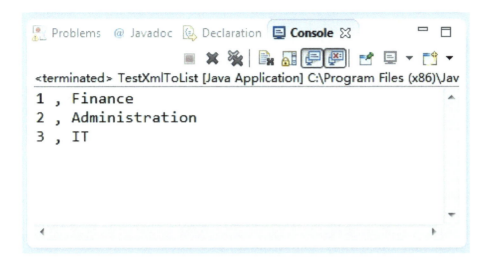

Java Reflection

1. Create a model class: com.entity.Product.java

```java
package com.entity;

public class Product {
    private int id;
    private String name;
    private int quantity;
    private double price;

    public Product(int id, String name, int quantity, double price) {
        super();
        this.id = id;
        this.name = name;
        this.quantity = quantity;
        this.price = price;
    }

    public Product() {
        super();
        this.id = 100;
        System.out.println("Product construction method is called");
    }

    public int getId() {
        return id;
    }

    public void setId(int id) {
        this.id = id;
    }

    public String getName() {
        return name;
    }

    public void setName(String name) {
        this.name = name;
    }
```

```java
    public int getQuantity() {
        return quantity;
    }

    public void setQuantity(int quantity) {
        this.quantity = quantity;
    }

    public double getPrice() {
        return price;
    }

    public void setPrice(double price) {
        this.price = price;
    }
}
```

2. Create a TestReflectionInstantiation.java , Reflection instantiation

```java
package com.reflection;

public class TestReflectionInstantiation {

   public static void main(String[] args) {
      try {
         Class clazz = Class.forName("com.entity.Product");

         //Instantiation
         Object obj = clazz.newInstance();

      } catch (Exception e) {
         e.printStackTrace();
      }
   }
}
```

Result:

3. Create a TestGetMemberVariable.java , get member variables name and type

```java
package com.reflection;

import java.lang.reflect.Field;

public class TestGetMemberVariable {
    public static void main(String[] args) {
        try {
            Class clazz = Class.forName("com.entity.Product");
            Object obj = clazz.newInstance();

            //Get all member variables
            Field[] fields = clazz.getDeclaredFields();
            for (Field field : fields) {

                String name = field.getName(); //The name of the field
                String typeName = field.getType().getName();  //The type of the field

                System.out.println(typeName + " " + name);
            }
        } catch (Exception e) {
            e.printStackTrace();
        }
    }
}
```

Result:

```
Problems  @ Javadoc  Declaration  Console 

<terminated> TestGetMemberVariable [Java Application] C:\Program File
Product construction method is called
int id
java.lang.String name
int quantity
double price
```

27

4. Create a TestMethodInvoke.java , method call

```java
package com.reflection;

import java.lang.reflect.Method;

public class TestMethodInvoke {
    public static void main(String[] args) {
        try {
            Class clazz = Class.forName("com.entity.Product");
            Object obj = clazz.newInstance();

            //Reflect to call method by  name
            Method method = clazz.getMethod("getId", null);
            Object result = method.invoke(obj, null);

            System.out.println(result);
        } catch (Exception e) {
            e.printStackTrace();
        }
    }
}
```

Result:

```
Problems   @ Javadoc   Declaration   Console ⊠

<terminated> TestMethodInvoke [Java Application] C:\Program Files (x86
Product construction method is called
100
```

5. Create a TestMethodParameter.java , method call with parameter

```java
package com.reflection;

import java.lang.reflect.Method;

public class TestMethodParameter {
    public static void main(String[] args) {
        try {
            Class clazz = Class.forName("com.entity.Product");
            Object obj = clazz.newInstance();

            //Calling a method with parameters setName
            Method method = clazz.getMethod("setName", new Class[] { String.class });
            Object result = method.invoke(obj, new Object[] { "Easy Learning Java" });

            //Calling a method getName
            method = clazz.getMethod("getName", null);
            result = method.invoke(obj, null);

            System.out.println(result);

        } catch (Exception e) {
            e.printStackTrace();
        }
    }
}
```

Result:

```
Problems  @ Javadoc  Declaration  Console
<terminated> TestMethodParameter [Java Application] C:\Program Files
Product construction method is called
Easy Learning Java
```

Convert Any Object to XML

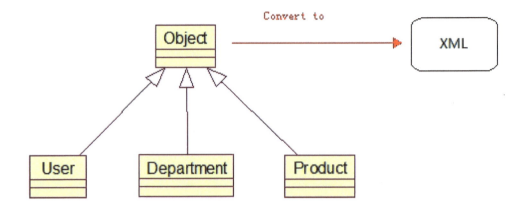

1. Create a model class: com.entity.User.java

```java
package com.entity;

public class User {
    private int id;
    private String username;
    private String pwd;

    public User() {
    }

    public User(int id, String username, String pwd) {
        super();
        this.id = id;
        this.username = username;
        this.pwd = pwd;
    }

    public int getId() {
        return id;
    }

    public void setId(int id) {
        this.id = id;
    }

    public String getUsername() {
        return username;
    }

    public void setUsername(String username) {
        this.username = username;
    }

    public String getPwd() {
        return pwd;
    }

    public void setPwd(String pwd) {
        this.pwd = pwd;
    }
}
```

2. Create a test class: com.xml5.TestObjectToXml

```java
package com.xml5;

import java.lang.reflect.*;
import com.entity.*;

public class TestObjectToXml {
    public static void main(String[] args) {

        User user = new User(1, "admin", "111111");
        System.out.println(ObjectToXml(user));

        System.out.println("----------------------------------------");

        Department dept = new Department(1, "Information Technology");
        System.out.println(ObjectToXml(dept));

        System.out.println("----------------------------------------");

        Product product = new Product(1, "Easy Learning Python 3",1000,3.99);
        System.out.println(ObjectToXml(product));
    }
```

```java
//Pass any object to generate the xml string
public static String ObjectToXml(Object obj) {
    StringBuilder sb = new StringBuilder();
    try {
        Class clazz = obj.getClass();
        String className = clazz.getSimpleName(); //Get the class name
        Field[] fields = clazz.getDeclaredFields(); //Get all member variables of an object

        sb.append("<?xml version=\"1.0\" encoding=\"UTF-8\"?>\n");
        sb.append("<data>\n");
        sb.append(" <" + className + ">\n");
        for (int i = 0; i < fields.length; i++) {
            Field field = fields[i];
            String fieldName = field.getName(); //Get the field name

            // call method by method name
            String firstLetter = fieldName.substring(0, 1).toUpperCase();
            String leftLetter = fieldName.substring(1);
            Method method = clazz.getDeclaredMethod("get" + firstLetter + leftLetter, null);
            sb.append("  <" + fieldName + ">" + method.invoke(obj, null) + "</" + fieldName
+ ">\n");
        }
        sb.append(" </" + className + ">\n");
        sb.append("</data>");
    } catch (Exception e) {
        e.printStackTrace();
    }

    return sb.toString();
}
}
```

Result:

```
Problems  @ Javadoc  Declaration  Console ✕          ▼ ▭ ⊟

<terminated> TestObjectToXml [Java Application] C:\Program Files
<?xml version="1.0" encoding="UTF-8"?>
<data>
 <User>
   <id>1</id>
   <username>admin</username>
   <pwd>111111</pwd>
 </User>
</data>
------------------------------------------
<?xml version="1.0" encoding="UTF-8"?>
<data>
 <Department>
   <id>1</id>
   <name>Information Technology</name>
 </Department>
</data>
------------------------------------------
<?xml version="1.0" encoding="UTF-8"?>
<data>
 <Product>
   <id>1</id>
   <name>Easy Learning Python 3</name>
   <quantity>1000</quantity>
   <price>3.99</price>
 </Product>
</data>
```

Convert Any List to XML

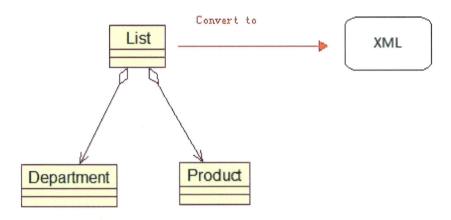

1. Create a test class: com.xml5.TestListToXml

```java
package com.xml5;

import java.lang.reflect.*;
import java.util.*;

import com.entity.Product;
import com.entity.User;

public class TestListToXml {
    public static void main(String[] args) {
        List<Product> productList = new ArrayList<Product>();
        productList.add(new Product(1, "Life is not limited",800,19.00));
        productList.add(new Product(2, "Easy Learning Javascript",900,3.99));
        System.out.println(ListToXml(productList));

        System.out.println("---------------------------------------------");

        List<User> userList = new ArrayList<User>();
        userList.add(new User(1, "David","111111"));
        userList.add(new User(2, "Grace","222222"));
        System.out.println(ListToXml(userList));
    }
```

```java
public static String ListToXml(List list) {
    StringBuilder sb = new StringBuilder();
    try {
        sb.append("<?xml version=\"1.0\" encoding=\"UTF-8\"?>\n");
        sb.append("<data>\n");
        for (int k = 0; k < list.size(); k++) {
            Object obj = list.get(k);
            Class clazz = obj.getClass();

            String className = clazz.getSimpleName();  //Get the class name
            //Get all member variables of the object
            Field[] fields = clazz.getDeclaredFields();
            sb.append(" <" + className + ">\n");
            for (int i = 0; i < fields.length; i++) {
                Field field = fields[i];
                // call method by method name
                String fieldName = field.getName();
                String firstLetter = fieldName.substring(0, 1).toUpperCase();
                String leftLetter = fieldName.substring(1);
                Method method = clazz.getDeclaredMethod("get" + firstLetter + leftLetter, null);
                sb.append("   <" + fieldName + ">" + method.invoke(obj, null) + "</" +
fieldName + ">\n");
            }
            sb.append(" </" + className + ">\n");

        }
        sb.append("</data>");
    } catch (Exception e) {
        e.printStackTrace();
    }
    return sb.toString();
  }
}
```

Result:

```
Problems  @ Javadoc  Declaration  Console ⊠           ⊐  ∂

<terminated> TestListToXml [Java Application] C:\Program Files (x

<?xml version="1.0" encoding="UTF-8"?>
<data>
 <Product>
   <id>1</id>
   <name>Life is not limited</name>
   <quantity>800</quantity>
   <price>19.0</price>
 </Product>
 <Product>
   <id>2</id>
   <name>Easy Learning Javascript</name>
   <quantity>900</quantity>
   <price>3.99</price>
 </Product>
</data>
---------------------------------------------
<?xml version="1.0" encoding="UTF-8"?>
<data>
 <User>
   <id>1</id>
   <username>David</username>
   <pwd>111111</pwd>
 </User>
 <User>
   <id>2</id>
   <username>Grace</username>
   <pwd>222222</pwd>
 </User>
</data>
```

Convert XML to Object

```xml
<?xml version="1.0" encoding="UTF-8"?>
<data>
    <user>
        <id>1</id>
        <username>admin</username>
        <pwd>111111</pwd>
    </user>
</data>
```

```xml
<?xml version="1.0" encoding="UTF-8"?>
<data>
    <product>
        <id>1</id>
        <name>Easy Learning C#</name>
        <quantity>800</quantity>
        <price>3.99</price>
    </product>
</data>
```

Convert to → Object

User

Product

1. Create a test class: com.xml6.TestXmlToObject

```java
package com.xml6;
import java.lang.reflect.*;
import java.util.*;
import org.dom4j.*;
import com.entity.Product;
import com.entity.User;

public class TestXmlToObject {
    public static void main(String[] args) {
        StringBuilder sb = new StringBuilder();

        sb.append("<?xml version=\"1.0\" encoding=\"UTF-8\"?>");
        sb.append("<data>");
        sb.append("   <user>");
        sb.append("       <id>1</id>");
        sb.append("       <username>admin</username>");
        sb.append("       <pwd>111111</pwd>");
        sb.append("   </user>");
        sb.append("</data>");
        User user = (User) XmlToObject(sb.toString(), User.class);
        System.out.println(user.getId() + "," + user.getUsername() + "," + user.getPwd());

        System.out.println("----------------------------------------");

        sb.delete(0, sb.length());
        sb.append("<?xml version=\"1.0\" encoding=\"UTF-8\"?>");
        sb.append("<data>");
        sb.append("   <product>");
        sb.append("       <id>1</id>");
        sb.append("       <name>Easy Learning C#</name>");
        sb.append("       <quantity>800</quantity>");
        sb.append("       <price>3.99</price>");
        sb.append("   </product>");
        sb.append("</data>");
        Product product = (Product) XmlToObject(sb.toString(), Product.class);
        System.out.println(product.getId() + "," + product.getName() + "," +
product.getQuantity()+","+product.getPrice());

    }
```

39

```java
public static Object XmlToObject(String xml, Class clazz) {
    Object obj = null;
    try {
        obj = clazz.newInstance();
        String className = clazz.getSimpleName().toLowerCase();
        Field[] fields = clazz.getDeclaredFields();

        Document doc = DocumentHelper.parseText(xml);
        List<Element> elementList = doc.selectNodes("/data/" + className);
        for (int i = 0; i < elementList.size(); i++) {
            Element element = elementList.get(i);

            Iterator<Element> elementIter = element.elementIterator();
            while (elementIter.hasNext()) {
                Element childElement = elementIter.next();
                String tag = childElement.getName();

                //Judge the tag equal to one of the fields
                for (int j = 0; j < fields.length; j++) {
                    Field field = fields[j];
                    String fieldName = field.getName();
                    if (tag.equals(fieldName)) {
                        String firstLetter = fieldName.substring(0, 1).toUpperCase();
                        String leftLetter = fieldName.substring(1);
                        Method method = null;
                        //Determine the type of parameter
                        if ("int".equals(field.getType().getName())) {
                            method = clazz.getMethod("set" + firstLetter + leftLetter, new Class[] {
int.class });
                            method.invoke(obj, new Object[] {
Integer.parseInt(childElement.getText()) });
                        }
                        if ("java.lang.String".equals(field.getType().getName())) {
                            method = clazz.getMethod("set" + firstLetter + leftLetter, new Class[] {
String.class });
                            method.invoke(obj, new Object[] { childElement.getText() });
                        }
                    }
                }
            }
        }
    } catch (Exception e) {
        e.printStackTrace();
    }
```

```
        return obj;
    }
}
```

Result:

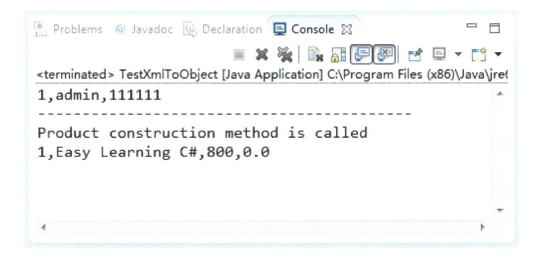

Convert XML to List

xml/user.xml

```xml
<?xml version="1.0" encoding="UTF-8"?>
<data>
    <user>
        <id>1</id>
        <username>David</username>
        <pwd>111111</pwd>
    </user>
    <user>
        <id>2</id>
        <username>Grace</username>
        <pwd>222222</pwd>
    </user>
</data>
```

Convert to

List

xml/product.xml

```xml
<?xml version="1.0" encoding="UTF-8"?>
<data>
    <product>
        <id>1</id>
        <name>Easy Learning MySQL SQL</name>
        <quantity>600</quantity>
        <price>3.99</price>
    </product>
    <product>
        <id>2</id>
        <name>Strong Happy Family</name>
        <quantity>800</quantity>
        <price>9.99</price>
    </product>
</data>
```

User   Product

1. Create a xml file : xml/user.xml

```xml
<?xml version="1.0" encoding="UTF-8"?>

<data>
  <user>
    <id>1</id>
    <username>David</username>
    <pwd>111111</pwd>
  </user>
  <user>
    <id>2</id>
    <username>Grace</username>
    <pwd>222222</pwd>
  </user>
</data>
```

2. Create a xml file : xml/product.xml

```xml
<?xml version="1.0" encoding="UTF-8"?>

<data>
  <product>
    <id>1</id>
    <name>Easy Learning MySQL SQL</name>
    <quantity>600</quantity>
    <price>3.99</price>
  </product>
  <product>
    <id>2</id>
    <name>Strong Happy Family</name>
    <quantity>800</quantity>
    <price>9.99</price>
  </product>
</data>
```

3. Create a test class: com.xml6.TestXmlToList

```java
package com.xml6;

import java.io.*;
import java.lang.reflect.*;
import java.util.*;
import org.dom4j.*;
import com.entity.Product;
import com.entity.User;

public class TestXmlToList {

    public static void main(String[] args) {

        String userXml=readXmlFile("xml/user.xml");
        List<User> userList = XmlToList(userXml, User.class);
        for (User item : userList) {
            System.out.println(item.getId() + "," + item.getUsername() + "," + item.getPwd());
        }

        System.out.println("----------------------------------------");

        String productXml=readXmlFile("xml/product.xml");
        List<Product> productList = XmlToList(productXml, Product.class);
        for (Product item : productList) {
            System.out.println(item.getId() + "," + item.getName() + "," +
item.getQuantity()+","+item.getPrice());
        }

    }
```

```java
public static String readXmlFile(String filePath) {
    BufferedReader br = null;
    StringBuffer sb = new StringBuffer();
    try {
        br = new BufferedReader(new FileReader(filePath));
        String line = null;
        while ((line = br.readLine()) != null) {
            sb.append(line);
        }
    } catch (Exception e1) {
        e1.printStackTrace();
    } finally {
        try {
            if (br != null) {
                br.close();
            }
        } catch (IOException e) {
            e.printStackTrace();
        }
    }

    return sb.toString();
}
```

```java
    public static List XmlToList(String xml, Class clazz) {
        List list = new ArrayList();
        Object obj = null;
        try {
            String className = clazz.getSimpleName().toLowerCase();
            Field[] fields = clazz.getDeclaredFields();

            Document doc = DocumentHelper.parseText(xml);
            List<Element> elementList = doc.selectNodes("/data/" + className);
            for (int i = 0; i < elementList.size(); i++) {
                Element element = elementList.get(i);
                obj = clazz.newInstance();

                Iterator<Element> elementIter = element.elementIterator();
                while (elementIter.hasNext()) {
                    Element childElement = elementIter.next();
                    String tag = childElement.getName();

                    for (int j = 0; j < fields.length; j++) {
                        Field field = fields[j];
                        String fieldName = field.getName();
                        if (tag.equals(fieldName)) {
                            String firstLetter = fieldName.substring(0, 1).toUpperCase();
                            String leftLetter = fieldName.substring(1);
                            Method method = null;
                            //Determine the type of parameter
                            if ("int".equals(field.getType().getName())) {
                                method = clazz.getMethod("set" + firstLetter + leftLetter, new Class[] {
int.class });
                                method.invoke(obj, new Object[] {
Integer.parseInt(childElement.getText()) });
                            }
                            if ("java.lang.String".equals(field.getType().getName())) {
                                method = clazz.getMethod("set" + firstLetter + leftLetter, new Class[] {
String.class });
                                method.invoke(obj, new Object[] { childElement.getText() });
                            }
                        }
                    }
                }
                list.add(obj);
            }
        } catch (Exception e) {
            e.printStackTrace();
```

```
        }
    return list;
    }
}
```

Result:

Parse JSON Object String

1. Download the jar package for parsing XML

json.jar

http://en.verejava.com/download.jsp?id=1

2. Add json.jar to Java Project

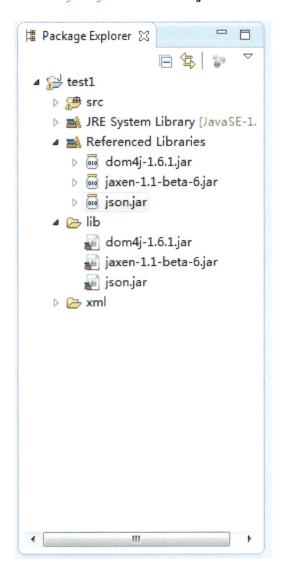

3. Create com.json1.Test

Parse and print the following JSON string key=value

{name: 'David', age: 25, marriage: true, money: 1000.5}

```java
package com.json1;
import org.json.*;
public class Test {

    public static void main(String[] args) {
        try {
            String person = "{name:'David',age:25,marriage:true,money:1000.5}";

            JSONObject jsonObj = new JSONObject(person);
            //Get the value by key
            String name = jsonObj.getString("name");
            int age = jsonObj.getInt("age");
            boolean marriage = jsonObj.getBoolean("marriage");
            double money = jsonObj.getDouble("money");

            System.out.println(name + "," + age + "," + marriage + "," + money);

        } catch (JSONException e) {
            e.printStackTrace();
        }
    }
}
```

Result:

```
Problems  @ Javadoc  Declaration  Console

<terminated> Test (29) [Java Application] C:\Program Files (x86)\Java\jre6\bin\java

David,25,true,1000.5
```

49

Parse Nested JSON Object

1. Create com.json2.Test

Parse and print the following JSON string key=value

{name:'David',age:25,address:{city:'Sanfrancisco',street:'Market',no:205}}

```java
import org.json.*;
public class Test {
    public static void main(String[] args) {
        try {
            String person =
"{name:'David',age:25,address:{city:'Sanfrancisco',street:'Market',no:205}}";
            JSONObject jsonObj = new JSONObject(person);
            String name = jsonObj.getString("name");
            int age = jsonObj.getInt("age");

            JSONObject addressObj = jsonObj.getJSONObject("address");
            String city = addressObj.getString("city");
            String street = addressObj.getString("street");
            int floor = addressObj.getInt("no");

            System.out.println(name);
            System.out.println(age);
            System.out.println("Adress:" + city + " " + street + " " + floor);
        } catch (JSONException e) {
            e.printStackTrace();
        }
    }
}
```

Result:

```
Problems  @ Javadoc  Declaration  Console

<terminated> Test (30) [Java Application] C:\Program Files (x86)\Java\jre6\bin\java

David
25
Adress:Sanfrancisco Market 205
```

Parse JSON Array String

1. Create com.json3.Test

Parse and print the following JSON Array string

['Basketball', 'Soccer', 'Rugby', 'Baseball', 'Billiards', 'Golf']

```java
import org.json.*;
public class Test {
    public static void main(String[] args) {
    try {
        String balls = "['Basketball', 'Soccer', 'Rugby', 'Baseball', 'Billiards', 'Golf']";

        JSONArray jsonArray = new JSONArray(balls);

        for (int i = 0; i < jsonArray.length(); i++) {
            String value = jsonArray.getString(i);
            System.out.println(value);
        }
    } catch (JSONException e) {
        e.printStackTrace();
    }
    }
}
```

Result:

```
Problems  @ Javadoc  Declaration  Console ⊠

<terminated> Test (31) [Java Application] C:\Program Files (x86)\Java\jre6\bin\java
Basketball
Soccer
Rugby
Baseball
Billiards
Golf
```

Parse 2D JSON Array

1. Create com.json4.Test

Parse and print the following JSON Array string

[['Tennis', 'Billiards', 'Golf'], ['Football', 'Rugby', 'Baseball']]

```java
import org.json.*;
public class Test {
  public static void main(String[] args) {
    String str = "[['Tennis', 'Billiards', 'Golf'], ['Football', 'Rugby', 'Baseball']]";

    try {
      JSONArray jsonArray = new JSONArray(str);
      for (int i = 0; i < jsonArray.length(); i++) {
        JSONArray childArray = jsonArray.getJSONArray(i);

        for (int j = 0; j < childArray.length(); j++) {
          String value = childArray.getString(j);
          System.out.print(value + " ");
        }
        System.out.println("");
      }
    } catch (JSONException e) {
      e.printStackTrace();
    }
  }
}
```

Result:

```
Problems   @ Javadoc   Declaration   Console ⌗

<terminated> Test (32) [Java Application] C:\Program Files (x86)\Java\jre6\bin\java
Tennis Billiards Golf
Football Rugby Baseball
```

Parse JSON Object Array

1. Create com.json6. Test

Parse and print the following JSON Array string

[{start:'Beijing',end:'Shanghai',price:100},{start:'Tokyo',end:'London',price:900},{start:'New York',end:'Los Angeles',price:300}]

```java
import org.json.*;
public class Test {
    public static void main(String[] args) {
        String ticketList =
"[{start:'Beijing',end:'Shanghai',price:100},{start:'Tokyo',end:'London',price:900},{start:'New York',end:'Los Angeles',price:300}]";

        try {
            JSONArray jsonArray = new JSONArray(ticketList);
            for (int i = 0; i < jsonArray.length(); i++) {
                JSONObject jsonObj = jsonArray.getJSONObject(i);
                String start = jsonObj.getString("start");
                String end = jsonObj.getString("end");
                int price = jsonObj.getInt("price");
                System.out.println(start + "," + end + "," + price);
            }
        } catch (JSONException e) {
            e.printStackTrace();
        }
    }
}
```

Result:

```
Problems  @ Javadoc  Declaration  Console ✕

<terminated> Test (33) [Java Application] C:\Program Files (x86)\Java\jre6\bin\jav:
Beijing,Shanghai,100
Tokyo,London,900
New York,Los Angeles,300
```

Object to JSONObject

1. Create com.json7.Test

```java
import org.json.JSONObject;
import com.entity.*;
public class Test {
    public static void main(String[] args) {

        Department dept = new Department(1, "Finance");
        JSONObject jsonObj = new JSONObject(dept);
        System.out.println(jsonObj.toString());

        System.out.println("-----------------------------------------");

        User user = new User(1, "David","111111");
        JSONObject jsonObj2 = new JSONObject(user);
        System.out.println(jsonObj2.toString());

        System.out.println("-----------------------------------------");

        Product product = new Product(1, "Best Life",1000,29);
        JSONObject jsonObj3 = new JSONObject(product);
        System.out.println(jsonObj3.toString());
    }
}
```

Result:

```
Problems  @ Javadoc  Declaration  Console ✕

<terminated> Test (34) [Java Application] C:\Program Files (x86)\Java\jre6\bin\javaw.exe
{"id":1,"name":"Finance"}
-----------------------------------------
{"id":1,"pwd":"111111","username":"David"}
-----------------------------------------
{"id":1,"price":29,"name":"Best Life","quantity":1000}
```

Array to JSONArray

1. Create com.json8.Test

```java
package com.json8;

import org.json.JSONArray;
import org.json.JSONException;

public class Test {
  public static void main(String[] args) {

    String[] colors = { "Red", "Blue", "Green" };

    try {

      JSONArray jsonArray = new JSONArray(colors);
      System.out.println(jsonArray.toString());

    } catch (JSONException e) {
      e.printStackTrace();
    }
  }
}
```

Result:

| Problems | @ Javadoc | Declaration | Console ⊠ |

```
<terminated> Test (35) [Java Application] C:\Program Files (x86)\Java\jre6\bin\javaw.exe
["Red","Blue","Green"]
```

Map to JSONObject

1. Create com.json9.Test

```java
package com.json9;

import java.util.*;
import org.json.JSONObject;
import com.entity.*;

public class Test {
  public static void main(String[] args) {

    Map map = new HashMap();
    map.put("username", "David");
    map.put("password", "111111");
    map.put("telephone", "415232323");
    map.put("department", new Department(1,"Finance"));
    map.put("product", new Product(1,"Strong Happy Family",100,9.9));

    JSONObject jsonObj = new JSONObject(map);

    System.out.println(jsonObj.toString());
  }
}
```

Result:

```
{"product":{"id":1,"price":9.9,"name":"Strong Happy
Family","quantity":100},"username":"David","department":{"id":1,"name":"Finance"},"passw
ord":"111111","telephone":"415232323"}
```

List to JSON Object Array

1. Create com.json10.Test

```java
package com.json10;

import java.util.*;
import org.json.JSONArray;
import com.entity.*;

public class Test {
    public static void main(String[] args) {

        List list = new ArrayList();
        list.add(60);
        list.add("Easy Learning Oracle SQL");
        list.add(new User(1,"David","111111"));
        list.add(new Department(1,"Technology"));
        list.add(new Product(1,"Easy Learning Python 3",1000,3.99));

        JSONArray jsonArray = new JSONArray(list);
        System.out.println(jsonArray.toString());
    }
}
```

Result:

```
[60,"Easy Learning Oracle
SQL",{"id":1,"pwd":"111111","username":"David"},{"id":1,"name":"Technology"},{"id":1,"price":3.99,"name":"Easy Learning Python 3","quantity":1000}]
```

Thanks for learning

https://www.amazon.com/dp/B08HTXMXVY   https://www.amazon.com/dp/B086SPBJ87

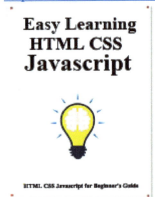
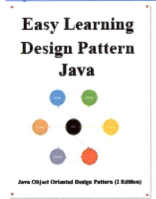

https://www.amazon.com/dp/B08BWT6RCT

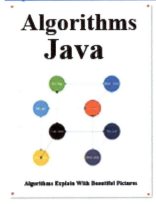

www.ingramcontent.com/pod-product-compliance
Lightning Source LLC
Chambersburg PA
CBHW041428050326
40689CB00003B/702